CENGAGE Learning

Poetry for Students, Volume 33

Project Editor: Sara Constantakis Rights Acquisition and Management: Margaret Abendroth, Margaret Chamberlain-Gaston, Sara Crane, Robyn Young Composition: Evi Abou-El-Seoud Manufacturing: Drew Kalasky

Imaging: John Watkins

Product Design: Pamela A. E. Galbreath, Jennifer Wahi Content Conversion: Katrina Coach Product Manager: Meggin Condino

For product information and technology assistance, contact us at **Gale Customer Support, 1-800-877-4253.**

For permission to use material from this text or product, submit all requests online at **www.cengage.com/permissions.**

Further permissions questions can be emailed to **permissionrequest@cengage.com** While every effort has been made to ensure the reliability of the information presented in this publication, Gale, a part of Cengage Learning, does not guarantee the accuracy of the data contained herein. Gale accepts no payment for listing; and inclusion in the publication of any organization, agency, institution, publication, service, or individual does not imply endorsement of the editors or publisher. Errors brought to the attention of the publisher and verified to the satisfaction of the publisher will be corrected in future editions.

Gale
27500 Drake Rd.
Farmington Hills, MI, 48331-3535

ISBN-13: 978-1-4144-4181-8
ISBN-10: 1-4144-4181-9
ISSN 1094-7019

This title is also available as an e-book.
ISBN-13: 978-1-4144-4954-8

ISBN-10: 1-4144-4954-2
Contact your Gale, a part of Cengage Learning sales
representative for ordering information.

Printed in the United States of America
1 2 3 4 5 6 7 14 13 12 11 10

Sympathy

Paul Laurence Dunbar 1899

Introduction

"Sympathy" was published in *Lyrics of the Hearthside* (1899), Paul Laurence Dunbar's fourth book of poems, one of the six major volumes he would complete in his brief thirty-three years of life. Though he also wrote novels, short stories, songs, and plays, he is remembered chiefly as a poet. Before writing "Sympathy," he was already famous and known as the Negro Poet Laureate, having toured the country performing his dialect poems about the plantation days. By 1899, the year "Sympathy" was published, he was discouraged that the public did not seem interested in his other works written in standard English. He wrote his serious poetry, like "Sympathy," in literary English, on a variety of subjects in addition to black themes. He had a lyric gift, but critics said his standard English poems were imitative and praised only the poems in dialect, which they believed to be more genuinely expressive of the Negro. The poem "Sympathy" is one of his most famous statements about racism. He did not feel free to write as he wanted and compared the feeling to being a bird in a cage.

The son of slaves, Dunbar felt the continuing legacy of slavery in a time of rampant racism in the United States. Dunbar's struggle to become the first recognized African American author continued even after his death in 1906. Later readers accused him of catering to whites with his poems depicting slaves on the plantation. In the modern age, he has taken his place as one of the founders of African American literature, and his poems have been memorized by generations of African Americans and other Americans alike. Though he felt like a failure, he inspired the writers of the Harlem Renaissance in the 1920s to use their vernacular speech as literary expression. "Sympathy" can be found in the *Collected Poetry of Paul Laurence Dunbar* (1993), published by the University Press of Virginia.

Author Biography

Dunbar was born June 27, 1872, in Dayton, Ohio, to Joshua Dunbar and Matilda Burton Murphy Dunbar, a widow with two sons by her previous slave marriage. Dunbar's parents had both been slaves in Kentucky. After the emancipation, thousands of freed slaves moved north, and Matilda took her young sons to Dayton and became a laundry woman, until she met and married Joshua. Joshua was an alcoholic, and Matilda obtained a divorce and custody of Dunbar, her sickly son, of whom she was protective. Dunbar was the only black student at Dayton Central High School, but he was accepted and excelled.

Dunbar began to write seriously at the age of sixteen and published some of his poems locally. His first real encounter with racial discrimination came after high school in 1891. He could only find menial work as an elevator boy. However, when the Western Association of Writers met in Dayton in 1892, Dunbar was invited to give the welcome, which he composed and recited in verse. He made such a positive impression on the group that he found supporters to help him publish his first collection of poetry, *Oak and Ivy*, in 1892. The volume contains black dialect poems inspired by the dialect work of James Whitcomb Riley. In 1893, Dunbar went to Chicago, Illinois, to work at the Haitian Pavilion at the Columbian Exposition. There he met abolitionist and author Frederick

Douglass who recognized his talent and employed him.

With the help of patrons, Dunbar published his second volume, *Majors and Minors*, in 1896. It was favorably reviewed in *Harper's Weekly* by William Dean Howells, a leading American writer and critic at the time. Dunbar became an overnight celebrity as the first nationally known black writer in American society. With his charm, manners, talent, and musical voice, his readings electrified audiences. In 1896, *Lyrics of a Lowly Life* was published by Dodd, Mead in New York.

In 1897 Dunbar worked as a clerk in the Library of Congress. He married another black author, Alice Ruth Moore in 1898 at the height of his fame and productivity. He published his first novel, *The Uncalled*, and first collection of short stories, *Folks from Dixie*, in that same year. *Lyrics of the Hearthside*, containing "Sympathy," was published in 1899.

Dunbar became gravely ill in 1899 with tuberculosis. The Dunbars moved to Denver, Colorado for his health, where he published his second novel, *The Love of Landry*, and a collection of short stories titled *The Strength of Gideon* in 1900. His third novel, *The Fanatics*, was published in 1901, and his last novel, *The Sport of the Gods*, was released in 1902.

Also in 1902, Dunbar and Moore separated because of his alcoholism. He spent his last days in Dayton with his mother, still producing until the end: *Lyrics of Love and Laughter* and *In Old Plantation Days* (both 1903); *The Heart of Happy Hollow* (1904); and *Lyrics of Sunshine and Shadow* (1905). He died of tuberculosis on February 9, 1906, at the age of thirty-three. Many of his poems, essays, and plays were collected and published posthumously.

Poem Summary

Stanza 1

LINES 1-3

"Sympathy" is a lyric in iambic tetrameter, seven line stanzas of four metric feet per line. The last line of each stanza is shorter, with three feet. The first line establishes the poem's controlling metaphor of the caged bird looking at a spring day, which mirrors the speaker's situation. The speaker ends the line with an exclamation that suggests a sigh of regret. Although the main rhythm of the poem is iambic (alternating unstressed and stressed beats), many spondees (two strong beats together) are used for emphasis.

The next few lines create a contrast between the cage and a beautiful spring day. The bird would especially feel restrained on a day when the sun is shining outside on the meadows and hills. In line 3, the image of wind blowing through fresh grass creates a feeling of refreshment and freedom, denied to the caged bird. The rhyme scheme of this stanza is *ABAABCC*. Lines 1, 3, and 4 are connected through end rhyme, which helps create the melodious singing sound of wind and the river in the next line. The alliteration (repetition of initial consonants) in lines 2, 3, 4, and 5, reinforces the flowing sounds of wind and water.

LINES 4-7

In line 4, the river, like the wind, is another image of movement. This dynamic quality of the landscape would make anyone inside a small space feel restless. The first bird singing in spring, depicted in line 5, and the first flower opening express hope ordinarily, but to one shut up, it would be torture not to share the joy of expansion, to be a mere onlooker.

The perfume from the flower is delicate and subtle, like a bird's song. The suggestion in line 6 that the perfume actually sneaks out of the flower cup when no one is looking (through alliteration) is another image of the natural expression of living things that cannot be denied or shut off. The thought breaks off with a dash creating suspense before the last line of the stanza. The expansion of the previous line is brought to a sudden halt in line 7 with the return to the image of the caged bird. The rhythm and rhyme of the poem establish the nature of life to sing out.

Media Adaptations

- *The Paul Laurence Dunbar Collection* is a package of three DVDs and three audiotapes with top African American storytellers reading stories and poems by the poet. It was produced by Cerebellum Corporation in 2008.

- *The Poetry of Paul Laurence Dunbar*, narrated by Bobby Norfolk, produced in 2004 by August House, is available as an audio download or audio CD from LearnOutLoud.com.

Stanza 2

LINES 8-10

In line 8, the speaker says he understands why the bird beats its wing inside the cage. The spondees emphasize the useless flapping of the bird's wings. In the next line, the bird continues hopelessly to beat its wings on the cage bars until it bleeds. The repeated alliteration in lines 8 and 9 create a feeling of restraint. The cage metaphor suggests the former slave status of black people, but it also signifies a current restraint. The poet's wife, Alice Dunbar, says he wrote the poem when he was working all day in the Library of Congress in Washington, D.C., looking out the barred windows to the green grass and trees. He felt imprisoned, doing menial work, when he wanted to be writing. In line 10, the bird flaps his wings but instead of getting anywhere, it must return to its perch. The spondee in the middle of the line recreates this image of the flapping wings pushing the bird back to its perch.

LINES 11-14

In line 11, the speaker expresses what the bird wants to do. Instead of clinging to a perch, it wants to be on the swinging branch of a tree. Both a perch and a bough are made of wood, but one is alive with movement, and one is dead and artificial as part of a man-made birdcage. It is apparent in line 12 that the bird has obviously repeated this action many times because it has scars from previous attempts to free itself from its cage. The fact that the scars are very old, however, could also suggest the legacy of slavery. The current pain of facing racism and restriction evokes the old historical wound that is still bleeding.

Each time the bird tries to get free and is thwarted, the pain in its wings hurts more. Line 13 ends with a dash, like hitting a brick wall. The pressure of the emotion has built up in this stanza without any resolution. To underscore this lack of movement, the concluding couplet is not CC but again, *AA* (the stanza's rhyme scheme is *ABAABAA*). Lines 8, 10, 11, 13, and 14 all rhyme. There are only two rhymes in this stanza, *A* and *B*, as though the bird is only allowed to sing one or two notes. Line 14 is a concluding shorter line and echoes line 8, which is a variation of the refrain of the poem.

Stanza 3

LINES 15-17

In line 15, the speaker says he understands why the bird in the cage sings, and again utters a sigh of sadness. The bird's wing is injured and its heart is sore, in line 16, and yet the bird sings. Its heart is not in the song, and yet it still sings. This is what people want from a caged bird: a song.

There is "B" alliteration in lines 16 and 17 as the speaker describes the bird once again beating his wings to get free. The "B" is a sound that stops as it is articulated. It suggests that the power of the bird's song is stifled. This line could also paradoxically explain the fact that the only freedom the bird or speaker feels is in singing, even if constrained.

LINES 18-21

Lines 15, 17, and 18 rhyme, but the lyrical effect is muted in this stanza, with darker images and harsher sounds. In line 18, the speaker says that the song the bird sings is not joyful. The song the bird sings is a spontaneous prayer from its heart. The feeling that the bird has reached its limit is recreated in the three strong beats together at the end of line 19.

In line 20, the bird's song is also described as a plea, a begging to a higher power for relief. This tentative prayer ends with a dash at the end of the line, showing that it is inconclusive. The rhyme scheme of this stanza is the same as the first stanza (*ABAABCC*). It explains that the speaker understands why the bird is singing despite its imprisonment.

Themes

Racism

The central metaphor of the caged bird in "Sympathy," with the bird forced to perform within confinement, could be taken as suggesting the slavery African Americans endured in the United States for two and a half centuries. Though Dunbar lived after the emancipation, the legacy of slavery continued through various social, legal, and psychological constraints. He was refused white collar or journalistic work because of his race, forced to work in the confinement of an elevator and the barred library stacks that were the inspiration for the poem. Dunbar was a brilliant and creative man, but he struggled to overcome the racial stereotype of blacks as slow, lazy, and child-like. The blacks he portrayed in his dialect poems, singing and dancing on the plantation, were part of the folklore of the past to him, like the Midwestern folklore used in James Whitcomb Riley's poems. He heard stories of the Old South from his mother and had a talent for reproducing accent, phrasing, and characterization. Dunbar was also highly educated. He saw himself as middle class, urbane, worldly, and able to meet other artists from around the world.

Though Dunbar never denied his race, and in fact, made many statements on racial injustice, he did not feel he should be tied down to black dialect poems. He was interested in art and experimented with many genres and ethnic voices. He used both white and black characters in his fiction. Dunbar wrote serious literary pieces in the tradition of Lord Alfred Tennyson, Henry Wadsworth Longfellow, John Keats, and Percy Bysshe Shelley. Dunbar became famous as an African American poet but few understood the range of his accomplishments or regarded his many talents as important. His dialect poems imitating the speech of southern plantation blacks were what made him popular, and people wanted to see him perform what they thought was authentic black speech. Like a bird in a cage, he felt he had to produce what audiences expected of a black man.

Topics for Further Study

- James Whitcomb Riley (1853-1916) was an influence on Dunbar's decision to write local color poems using dialect. Choose one student in class to recite Dunbar's dialect poem, "When De Co'n Pone's Hot," celebrating a Southern black meal. Another student can perform James Whitcomb Riley's Hoosier dialect poem, "When the Frost Is on the Punkin." Discuss the scenes and characterization of each poem in class. How do the poets preserve regional folk life in their poems?

- Alice Dunbar (later known as Dunbar-Nelson), the poet's wife, was also a well-known black author. Read Alice Dunbar's poems "Rainy Day" and "Cano—I Sing" and contrast the messages of those poems to Dunbar's "Sympathy." Write a paper comparing and contrasting their poems in content and style.

- Research the influence of Dunbar on poets of the Harlem Renaissance, such as Langston Hughes, and report to the class in a PowerPoint audio and visual presentation, using poem selections of both authors to illustrate your points.

- Dunbar's poems "Sympathy" and "We Wear the Mask" are often taken as statements of the difficulties

African Americans have faced. Use these poems as points of departure to critique the statement of another work of African American poetry or fiction of your choice in an essay.

- African American poetry is influenced by such oral forms as spirituals, sermons, jazz, work songs, gospel, and blues. Apply this idea to the dialect poems of Dunbar. First have the class read one of Dunbar's poems such as "An Antebellum Sermon" or "A Negro Love Song" on paper and then have it performed aloud by a practiced reader. In an in-class essay explain what you heard from the music and rhythm of the poems that you did not see while reading it on paper.

- Compare and contrast the theme of freedom in "Sympathy" with the freedom represented in the Pearl Buck novel *The Good Earth*, (1931) suitable for younger readers. Present your conclusions in an essay.

Dunbar never felt he had accomplished what he wanted. Critics have since interpreted his frustration in many ways; for instance, that he was unable to find an authentic black voice within white culture. The poem "Sympathy" is often taken as a statement of this dilemma, where the poet feels hemmed in and unable to be himself. The old scars that the bird carries from beating his wings on the bars could symbolize the scars of the black race that Dunbar also must carry, for though Dunbar lived a comparatively privileged life, moving freely in both black and white society, he was not free of being typecast. Similarly, much was expected of him as a symbol of his race. He was rarely allowed to be an individual publically. Other Dunbar poems that comment on racism include "The Haunted Oak," "We Wear the Mask," "The Poet," "Right's Security," "The Warrior's Prayer," "To the South on Its New Slavery," "Frederick Douglass," and "Ode to Ethiopia."

Freedom

A bird is a frequent poetic symbol for freedom since it can fly. It is also a common symbol in poetry for the poet. The yearning of the bird for its freedom in "Sympathy" is graphically portrayed when the bird sees the landscape outside. It hears other birds sing and the wind and river rushing and responds by beating its wings against the cage, trying to get out. The urge for freedom is so compelling that the bird endures pain again and again trying to fly, only to be beaten back. By presenting the contrast between the cage and the spring day, it is obvious that a cage is a cruel perversion of life. Whether meaning a literal cage, as slavery, or a psychological one, as Dunbar and many black artists have felt, Dunbar protests that it is wrong to thwart the potential of any living being. It is natural for every creature to express its life and want its freedom. In this poem, the bird, and by implication the speaker, is denied what is natural. The speaker has sympathy for the bird, so the poem is from the point of view of the one without freedom. An onlooker might think that the bird should be quiet, or that the speaker should be content. From the interior point of view, racial prejudice causes extreme suffering and damage. The poet emphasizes a sense of sympathy for the prisoner. Other Dunbar poems on the theme of freedom include "Emancipation," "Ode to Ethiopia," "Justice," "Differences," and "Lincoln."

The Nature of Poetry

Bird song is a metaphor for poetry. There are several implications about poetry in the poem. First, a poet is a person with sympathy. Sympathy means to feel with another being, to put oneself in the place of others. Dunbar's writings, both poetry and prose, do exhibit such sympathy with a variety of characters from all cultures. For instance, his short story "The Lynching of Jube Benson" shows insight into both black and white psychology. He depicts African Americans in his dialect poems with humor and insight ("The Party" and "When Malindy Sings").

Dunbar was influenced by Romantic literature for his serious poems and by regional local color writing for his dialect poems. His underlying aesthetic in the standard English verse is romantic in his choice of subject matter (love, great lives, art, freedom, injustice) and form (odes, ballads, sonnets, and lyrics). Romantic poets celebrated nature as Dunbar does in the first stanza of "Sympathy." The poet, being sensitive, feels with all creatures, and sees and records beauty as well as injustice. While in his fiction Dunbar experimented with realism, for instance in his novel *Sport of the Gods*; in his poetry he holds romantic tenets, showing his talent as a great lyricist.

Freedom is essential for creativity to flow. A bird may sing in a cage, but it is not the same as the bird singing unfettered in nature. In fact, one cannot put restraint on song, for it is a spontaneous welling up of the impulse of life. This is brought out in the first stanza with the image of the perfume sneaking out of the flower cup. It is so delicate an expression that one might hardly notice how the perfume is emitted, but certainly, one could not stop a flower from putting forth its scent. It is part of the identity of the flower. Similarly, it is in the nature of a bird to sing or a poet to write. One does not tell the river how to flow or the bird how to sing. When society shuts down creativity or the voice of anyone trying to speak his or her truth, it is against nature, the nature of the individual, and of nature in general.

The song of a bird or poet comes from a deep place. Whether in joy or pain, the poet/bird sings from the heart about the origin of its song. If restrained, the singer will not produce a happy song, but it is important to note that the desire to sing is so strong that even pain will not stop the singer from singing. In fact, it can make the song more poignant. This idea of the sorrow of African American song is inherent in the blues, and Dunbar believed that rich lyric sorrow was the essence of African music.

Style

Personal Lyric

Lyric poetry is an ancient genre, popular from classical times through the present, in almost every culture. Lyric means song and was originally a song sung to an accompanying lyre or stringed instrument. A lyric poem is short and musical rather than narrative or dramatic, expressing emotions or thoughts. A personal lyric represents the subjective experience of one speaker. The speaker may or may not have the same feelings as the poet, but it is the representation of a speaking person's thoughts on a particular subject, for instance, love. Dunbar was influenced by the lyric poetry of Tennyson, Keats, Shelley, Longfellow, and Edgar Allan Poe. Famous lyric poems include Tennyson's "Now the Crimson Petal Sleeps" and Poe's "To Helen."

The fact that lyrics predominate in Dunbar's poetry is illustrated by the fact that several of his volumes have the term lyric in the title: *Lyrics of Lowly Life*, *Lyrics of the Hearthside*, *Lyrics of Love and Laughter*, and *Lyrics of Sunshine and Shadow*. The lyric or song was flexible enough to accommodate both Dunbar's poems in literary English and his dialect poems. He put the two types side by side in the later volumes, so that one might see "In the Morning," written in humorous dialect, alongside the serious "The Poet," expressing in standard English his concern that he had failed as a writer.

Protest Poem

Dunbar was no doubt inspired by two of his favorite American poets, John Greenleaf Whittier and Longfellow, who wrote protest poems against slavery before the Civil War as part of the abolitionist movement. It was not necessary for Dunbar to depend on white models, however, for the history of African American oral traditions shows an emphasis on protest. The enslaved Africans kept up their spirits with encoded messages in their songs and spirituals. Such familiar religious spirituals as "Get on Board, Little Children" and "Go Down, Moses," were a way to talk about freedom and slavery in Biblical terms or to warn about an impending escape attempt. The song "Oh, Freedom" is another that was sung at secret meetings on the plantations. It became an anthem of the civil rights movement. The fact that these protests were coded indicates something important about early African American literature. It was dangerous to express protest too openly.

In the post-Reconstruction era, Dunbar was still writing in a time of racial tension. Like fiction writer Charles Waddell Chesnutt (1858-1932), Dunbar learned to write for a double audience, with protest generally muted or told through indirection. Some notable exceptions to this are Dunbar's famous racial assertions in "The Haunted Oak,"

"We Wear the Mask," and "Sympathy." "Sympathy" protests the racist conditions under which Dunbar had to write and live, though his argument is cleverly worded through metaphor. He symbolically refers to the pain of slavery that generations of Africans must still carry as the scars on the caged bird's wings. Those scars would be enumerated more bluntly in the protest poems of the Harlem Renaissance in the 1920s and 1930s in such examples as "Incident" and "Saturday's Child" by Countee Cullen. Langston Hughes's "I, Too, Sing America" asserts more boldly than Dunbar dared, that the black voice is part of the American voice.

The protest poems of the 1960s centered around the civil rights movement; for instance, "The Ballad of Birmingham" by Dudley Randall recounted the bombing of children in a church. Compared to the later more aggressive protest poems written by black poets, Dunbar has been accused by modern critics of being an Uncle Tom, accommodating white tastes with black stereotypes in his dialect poems. This is an incorrect assumption, for Dunbar did protest injustice in both his poetry and prose.

African American Poetry

Slave poets Lucy Terry, Jupiter Hammon, and Phillis Wheatley published works even before the American Revolution. Phillis Wheatley (1754-1784), the child prodigy slave of the Wheatley family who produced polished eighteenth-century verses, was the first well-known African American author, traveling abroad to promote her work and the work of abolitionists.

African American poetry refers to the writings of those people who were brought forcibly to the United States from Africa and kept in bondage for two and a half centuries. It was forbidden for slaves to learn to read or write, and yet they did both. At first they continued their native oral tradition with songs, spirituals, and sermons. After learning to write, many ex-slaves like Frederick Douglass wrote slave narratives.

During the post-Reconstruction era, from about 1870 to World War I, published black authors primarily produced journalistic prose or fiction, or single poems. Dunbar's ambition to be an accepted mainstream poet led him to write in standard European and American poetic forms. When inspired by James Whitcomb Riley's example to write poetry in regional dialect, he wrote poems in black southern dialect and became famous for it.

Dunbar preferred to write literary English poems, which he felt most expressed who he was. Yet his white audience felt his dialect poems expressed the authentic black experience and his publisher favored these works as well. Dunbar's dilemma was a crucial moment in the development of African American poetry. He wrote for two audiences with two different languages. "Sympathy" partly describes this dilemma of the black writer who writes against such a heavy burden of expectations.

Dunbar's experiments inspired later poets such as Hughes, James Weldon Johnson, Cullen, Claude McKay, and Jean Toomer during the Harlem Renaissance to integrate these separate modes of expression into an English language that could distinctively express the African American voice. It was the revolution of the 1960s that garnered African American literature, like other minority literatures, praise and respect. With black writers being taken seriously and winning Pulitzer and Nobel prizes, their work could no longer be denied its place as part of mainstream American literature, and black authors felt free to use whatever language their imaginations could invent.

Failure of Reconstruction

Reconstruction is the period after the Civil War (1865-1877) in which the United States tried to restructure American society by abolishing slavery and amending the Constitution (precisely the 13th, 14th, and 15th amendments) to give civil rights to four million former slaves. While federal troops were stationed in the South, state governments were organized to give blacks the right to vote and schools and positions in government. By 1877, however, white supremacists in the South had reasserted their power and states' rights to enact Jim Crow laws that led to segregation of the races and deprived blacks of their civil liberties. Peonage, the practice of creditors forcing debtors to work for them, was common in the South and was criticized in Dunbar's poem "To the South on Its New Slavery." Full citizenship for African Americans did not come about until almost a century later during the civil rights movement in the 1960s. Black historians have called the period from 1877 to the end of World War I the "nadir" of race relations in America.

Black Migration to Northern Cities

After the Civil War, the United States changed rapidly from an agrarian economy to industrial capitalism. With the emancipation, blacks began migrating from the South to escape poverty and racial violence to the North where there were jobs and more opportunities. The largest migrations happened after Dunbar's death, but even during his life he witnessed and even worried about African Americans moving from a country life in the South to ghettos in the northern cities. In *The Sport of the Gods*, he pictures a black family ruined by moving to New York. Dunbar was one of the first to see that racism could be as virulent in the North as in the South.

Compare & Contrast

- **1900:** Only a handful of African Americans, such as Alice Moore Dunbar, go to college.

  Today: Although underrepresented in terms of total college population, millions of African Americans enroll in higher education and earn college degrees.

- **1900:** There are few published African American writers, especially outside of black journals and magazines.

  Today: African American writers win the highest literary prizes (Pulitzer, Nobel), write best-selling novels that are made into films, and are studied as part of the American literary canon.

- **1900:** Jim Crow laws, which legally separate the races in public settings in southern states, regulate the lives of African Americans. These laws disenfranchise African Americans, who are not considered part of the democratic process.

  Today: African Americans have full political rights, and the first African American U.S. President, Barack Obama, is inaugurated in 2009.

- **1900:** Tuberculosis (TB), the cause of Dunbar's death, is almost always fatal, with no treatment available except bed rest in a mild climate.

  Today: TB can be cured with anti-TB drugs, although it has made a comeback recently, because it has become resistant to some traditional medications.

Racial Discrimination and Racial Violence

The terrorism the Ku Klux Klan and other hate groups inflicted on blacks in the late nineteenth and early twentieth century was largely countenanced by both southern and northern whites. D. W. Griffith's film *The Birth of a Nation*, released in 1915, clearly casts the Ku Klux Klan as heroes restoring order to the South and shows blacks as evil. W. E. B. Du Bois, the black activist whom Dunbar admired, objected to this piece of hate propaganda accepted as mainstream. In the 1890s, when Dunbar was beginning his career, there were hundreds of lynchings in the country. Dunbar was so appalled by this unpunished practice of mob violence that he wrote a poem, "The Haunted Oak," and the short story, "The Lynching of Jube Benson," in protest. Although Dunbar was luckier than many of his race, Dunbar did deal with racial discrimination, even in Ohio. He was unable to realize his dream of going to Harvard Law School and had to be satisfied with a high school education. He was forced into taking menial jobs and told flatly that newspapers and other businesses did not hire minorities.

Racial Stereotypes: Minstrelsy and Uncle Remus

Minstrel shows were a form of popular musical and comedy entertainment after the Civil War, lampooning blacks as stupid and superstitious. At first the parts were played by whites in blackface, but later, by blacks themselves in "Amos and Andy" routines, with stock characters like Jim Crow, Jim Dandy, and Mr. Bones. They sang and danced and spoke in southern black dialect. Even the most liberal newspapers and magazines of the day spread racist caricatures of African Americans in articles and cartoons. Popular myths about the "good old South" were spread in the Uncle Remus stories (1881) by a white journalist, Joel Chandler Harris, who used black folklore and dialect. As Dunbar also used life on the plantation and black dialect for his dialect poems, he was later criticized for portraying slavery in a comic and acceptable light. That this was not his intent or the result of his works has successfully been argued by many recent critics. The Uncle Remus stories were stereotypes; Dunbar's folk poems transcend such images.

Rise of the Black Middle Class

In spite of tremendous opposition, African Americans found ways to become educated and succeed, becoming lawyers, doctors, business entrepreneurs, actors, and artists. Dunbar is praised as the first black professional author in America, able to earn a living by writing and speaking. The strategy for raising blacks to the middle class was hotly debated among black activists. Booker T. Washington (1856-1915) was a slave, but he became an educator and leader of the African American community after the Civil War. He pleaded with middle-class whites to let the black race develop along separate lines to develop the industrial skills they needed to support themselves economically. He was accused later by W. E. B. Du Bois (1868-1963), a black scholar and political advocate, as an accommodationist (compromiser).

Though Washington won white support for blacks, he did not push for black college education and equal rights as Du Bois did.

Du Bois's famous statement that a black man lives in double consciousness, having to switch between white and black expectations, is often applied to Dunbar's situation of trying to please both white and black audiences. Du Bois was a founder of the National Association for the Advancement of Colored People (NAACP) and was the first African American to earn a Ph.D. from Harvard University. He began the push for civil rights which was later taken up by Dr. Martin Luther King, Jr.

In spite of Dunbar's early poverty, he grew up in a town that was more integrated than most. Dayton, Ohio, was an end point of the Underground Railroad and in Dunbar's youth, ten percent of the population was black. Dunbar graduated from a white high school, and he was even the editor of the school newspaper. He was proud to live a middle class life with his wife, Alice, in Washington, D.C., with other black professionals, a life he describes in his essay, "Negro Society in Washington" in the *Saturday Evening Post* (December 14, 1901). The black middle class at this point was still segregated, however.

Critical Overview

When Dunbar published his second collection of poems, *Majors and Minors* (1896), a famous actor, James Herne, sent his copy to novelist and critic William Dean Howells, who reviewed it in *Harper's Weekly* on June 27, 1896, reprinted in Peter Revell's *Paul Laurence Dunbar*. It was Dunbar's twenty-fourth birthday, and overnight he found himself famous as the first genuine Negro poet of America. Howells compares him to Robert Burns in his use of dialect, saying that Dunbar "has been able to bring us nearer to the heart of primitive human nature in his race than anyone else has yet done." Though Howells made Dunbar famous, the praise did a certain amount of damage, for Howells pronounces Dunbar's standard English poems to be inferior to his dialect pieces. Dunbar was never able to influence the public to take his standard English poems (such as "Sympathy"), or his prose, seriously. He established his fame as a performer of his dialect pieces.

When "Sympathy" was published in *Lyrics of the Hearthside* in 1899, critics echoed Howells's earlier statements. In a review for the *Baltimore Herald* (March, 1899) reprinted in E. W. Metcalf, Jr.'s *Paul Laurence Dunbar: A Bibliography*, a contributor comments: "Mr. Dunbar's choice of words is happier when he is writing in the musical speech of the Negro." Also reprinted in Metcalf's work, a contributor to the *New York Mail and*

Express (April 8, 1899) praises the standard English poems as "amateur excellence," but the dialect poems as proving "his eminence among the dialect writers of America." Many critics of the time saw his standard English poems as imitative.

After Dunbar's death, his widow, Alice Dunbar, also an author and critic, attempted to correct the idea that the dialect poems express the poet. Quoted by Revell in Twayne's "United States Author" series, Alice states: "it was in the pure English poems that the poet expressed *himself.* He may have expressed his race in the dialect poems; they were to him the side issues of his work." The controversy picked up in the 1920s with the new emphasis on black pride in the Harlem Renaissance making it appear that Dunbar catered to whites. According to Revell, Dunbar's friend and fellow writer James Weldon Johnson, in his anthology, *The Book of American Negro Poetry*, defends Dunbar as the first to use dialect "as a medium for the true interpretation of Negro character and psychology." In the first known balanced and serious criticism of Dunbar, *Paul Laurence Dunbar: Poet of His People* (1936), Benjamin Brawley claims that Dunbar was a genius who was constrained by the racism of his time from speaking as he wanted to, but also that he created a landmark for other black authors with his work.

Nevertheless, the 1940s and 1950s were low points in the appreciation of Dunbar. In *Dunbar Critically Examined* (1941), Victor Lawson declares: "In his poems in dialect Dunbar stood as the conscious or unconscious apologist of the plantation." This image of Dunbar was gradually erased with the revival of interest at the Centenary Conference on Dunbar in Dayton in 1972. In a contribution to *A Singer in the Dawn: Reinterpretations of Paul Laurence Dunbar* (1975), Darwin Turner provides an opinion similar to Howells's original evaluation: "[Dunbar's] unique contribution to American literature is his dialect poetry."

In hindsight, the criticism comes full circle, but with the addition of understanding both the racism Dunbar fought and his contribution of the black vernacular as legitimate poetic speech. In addition, new previously unpublished Dunbar manuscripts reveal his breadth and experimentation in various genres. Despite critical debates, Dunbar's poems entered the oral traditions of African Americans from the beginning, and they are often memorized by school children. In the 1980s, black poet Herbert Woodward Martin traveled with a one-man show, reciting Dunbar's dialect and standard poems to receptive audiences, illustrating their power when performed. Dunbar is now considered a mainstream American poet who was black, instead of a segregated Negro poet. This is what he had hoped for, but it took him a century to achieve this goal.

What Do I Read Next?

- *A Hope in the Unseen: An American Odyssey From the Inner City to the Ivy League* by Ron Suskind (Broadway Books, 1998) is a nonfiction book for young adults widely read in modern-day schools. Journalist Ron Suskind tracked the progress of Cedric Jennings out of an inner city high school in Washington, D.C., to Brown University. The work is the true story of how one courageous teenager fought his way out of poverty and violence to realize a dream that Dunbar was denied.

- The longest short story Dunbar ever wrote was originally published in *The Strength of Gideon* (1900).

"One Man's Fortune," reprinted in *The Paul Laurence Dunbar Reader* edited by Jay Martin and Gossie H. Hudson (Dodd, Mead, 1975) details the racist treatment of Bertram Halliday, a young black college graduate. In the story Dunbar demands equal treatment of blacks.

- *The Betrayal of the Negro: From Rutherford B. Hayes to Woodrow Wilson, Vol. 1* by Rayford Whittingham Logan, (Perseus, 1997) was first issued in 1954 and is a classic historical study of the racism of the post-Reconstruction era. A scholar at Howard University, Logan was in President Franklin D. Roosevelt's Black Cabinet.

- Young-adult novel *Mexican WhiteBoy* by Matt de la Pena (Delacorte, 2008) depicts biracial Danny Lopez's dilemma of not belonging to either the white American or Mexican culture. Dialogue includes street vernacular and Spanish words.

- *Give Us Each Day: The Diary of Alice Dunbar-Nelson*, edited by Gloria T. Hull (W.W. Norton, 1984), is the journal of Dunbar's widow for 1921 and 1926-1931. It gives a glimpse of the life of an intellectual black woman, writer, and political activist during the Harlem Renaissance.

- Jean Wagner and Kenneth Douglas's 1973 work *Black Poets of the United States: From Paul Laurence Dunbar to Langston Hughes* provides both a historical and biographical review of black poetry and major African American poets from early slavery to the Harlem Renaissance. Originally published in France in 1963, it provides a broad perspective.

Sources

Best, Felton O., *Crossing the Color Line: A Biography of Paul Laurence Dunbar 1872-1906*, Kendall/Hunt Publishers, 1996, pp. 44, 110.

Brawley, Benjamin, *Paul Lawrence Dunbar: Poet of His People*, University of North Carolina Press, 1936, reprint ed., Kennikat Press, 1967, pp. 4, 37, 76.

Braxton, Joanne M., Introduction to *The Collected Poetry of Paul Laurence Dunbar*, University Press of Virginia, 1993, p. xxi.

Dunbar, Paul Lawrence, "Negro in Literature," in *In His Own Voice: The Dramatic and Other Uncollected Works of Paul Laurence Dunbar*, edited by Herbert Woodward Martin and Ronald Primeau, Ohio University Press, 2002, pp. 206-207; originally published in *New York Commercial* 1898, Paul Laurence Dunbar Collection, reel IV, box 16, Ohio Historical Society.

———, "Negro Music," in *In His Own Voice: The Dramatic and Other Uncollected Works of Paul Laurence Dunbar*, edited by Herbert Woodward Martin and Ronald Primeau, Ohio University Press, 2002, pp. 184-85; originally published in *Chicago Record*, 1899, Paul Laurence Dunbar Collection, reel IV, box 18, Ohio Historical Society.

———, *The Collected Poetry of Paul Laurence Dunbar*, edited by Joanne M. Braxton, University

Press of Virginia, 1993.

————, *The Paul Laurence Dunbar Reader: A Selection of the Best of Paul Laurence Dunbar's Poetry and Prose, Including Writings Never Before Available in Book Form*, edited by Jay Martin and Gossie H. Hudson, Dodd, Mead, 1975.

Gates, Henry Louis, Jr., *Figures in Black: Words, Signs, and the "Racial" Self*, Oxford University Press, 1987, pp. 25-26, 29.

————, *The Signifying Monkey: A Theory of Afro-American Literary Criticism*, Oxford University Press, 1988, p. 66.

Gebhard, Caroline, "Inventing a 'Negro Literature': Race, Dialect, and Gender in the Early Work of Paul Laurence Dunbar, James Weldon Johnson, and Alice Dunbar-Nelson," in *Post-Bellum, Pre-Harlem: African American Literature and Culture 1877-1919*, edited by Barbara McCaskill and Caroline Gebhard, New York University Press, 2006, pp. 162-78.

Hudson, Gossie H., "The Crowded Years: Paul Laurence Dunbar in History," in *A Singer in the Dawn: Reinterpretations of Paul Laurence Dunbar*, edited by Jay Martin, Dodd, Mead, 1975, pp. 227-42.

Lawson, Victor, *Dunbar Critically Examined*, Associated Publishers, 1941, p. 78.

Metcalf, E. W., Jr., *Paul Laurence Dunbar: A Bibliography*, Scarecrow Press, 1975, pp. 131-33.

Revell, Peter, *Paul Laurence Dunbar*, Twayne's

"United States Author" series, No. 298, Twayne Publishers, 1979, pp. 90-91, 93, 190.

Roman, Camille, "The Caged Bird's Song and Its (Dis)Contents," in *Pacific Coast Philology*, Vol. 41, 2006, pp. 32-38.

Simon, Myron, "Dunbar and Dialect Poetry," in *A Singer in the Dawn: Reinterpretations of Paul Laurence Dunbar*, edited by Jay Martin, Dodd, Mead, 1975, p. 121.

Turner, Darwin T., "The Poet and the Myths," in *A Singer in the Dawn: Reinterpretations of Paul Laurence Dunbar*, edited by Jay Martin, Dodd, Mead, 1975, pp. 59-74.

Further Reading

Alexander, Eleanor, *Lyrics of Sunshine and Shadow: The Tragic Courtship and Marriage of Paul Laurence Dunbar and Alice Ruth Moore: A History of Love and Violence among the African American Elite*, New York University Press, 2001.

> Alexander chronicles the difficult marriage of the Dunbars and why they separated due to drinking and domestic violence. She also discusses other middle class African American marriages showing sociologically how the pressures of race and gender at the turn of the century eroded relationships.

Brown, Fahamisha Patricia, *Performing the Word: African American Poetry as Vernacular Culture*, Rutgers University Press, 1999.

> Brown focuses on the features of African American oral traditions that appear in vernacular speech and modern poetry. For instance, the call-and-response repetition, preaching, and the boast are highlighted in the works of various black poets.

Du Bois, W. E. B., *The Gift of Black Folk: The Negro in the Making of America*, 1924, Square One

Publishers, 2009.

> Sociologist, scholar, and civil rights activist Du Bois documents the contributions of African Americans in an attempt to counter negative stereotypes. He shows black Americans as explorers, inventors, artists, soldiers, and farmers. The book was reissued to mark the centennial of the National Association for the Advancement of Colored People, which Du Bois helped to found.

Dunbar, Paul Laurence, *The Sport of the Gods*, Dodd, Mead, 1902, Signet Classic, 1999.

> This realistic novel was ahead of its time in describing a southern black family moving to New York City and facing the same forces of racism as in the South because blacks had no legal protection.

Lightning Source UK Ltd.
Milton Keynes UK
UKHW020747131222
413853UK00014B/471